Charleston A to Z

By Rob Hicks

Illustrated by Cait Maloney

Island Media Publishing, LLC
120 N. 15th St.
Fernandina Beach, FL 32034
www.islandmediapublishing.com
Printed in China

ISBN 978-0-9829908-2-7
Library of Congress 2014901171

Island Media Publishing, LLC

For Jim and Lynn, two of South Carolina's
finest exports.
Rob Hicks

For my mom who always
said I could do it.
Cait Maloney

A is for abolition, a movement to set the slaves free,
but in Charleston the movement was hated
because the slaves' work was key.
In South Carolina the slaves were vital,
nowhere did they matter more,
so here the struggle for abolition would soon lead to the Civil War.

Abolition was a movement to end the slave trade and slavery. The idea gained momentum in America in the early 1800s, but many in the South were opposed to abolition. Slaves were very important to the Southern economy. They provided a free source of labor to man the fields and farms which produced crops the slaves' masters sold all over the country and the world. Obviously, the slave masters in the South enjoyed not having to pay their employees, and the buying and selling of slaves made some people a lot of money.

The slave trade was particularly profitable to the Port of Charleston, and the farms and plantations spread throughout South Carolina were very dependent on the work of slaves. Those in the North did not have the same dependency on slaves, however, and most who made the call for abolition lived there. There were many abolitionists in the South though, and their numbers grew along with the tension between them and slave owners. Eventually, South Carolina and Charleston realized that the United States would soon outlaw slavery, so they decided to secede from the Union. This helped spark the Civil War that would change America forever.

The bells of St. Michael's Episcopal Church are a favorite sound in Charleston. The eight bells in the tower originated in 1764. British soldiers confiscated them during the Revolutionary War and took them to England. They eventually found their way back to Charleston but were moved to Columbia during the Civil War for safe keeping. They were recast in their original foundry in England in 1866 and in 1993.

St. Michael's and its bells sit at the corner of Meeting and Broad Streets. This intersection is known as the Four Corners of Law. The intersection takes that nickname because it is said you can do anything that is legally required in life right here. At the church you can get married. Another corner has the oldest post office building in South Carolina where you can get your mail. One corner holds a courthouse where you can pay your taxes, and the last corner is home to Charleston's City Hall where you can deal with city business.

B is for the bells of St. Michael's, ringing out from a house of God
at one of the Four Corners of Law at the intersection of Meeting and Broad.
The four corners have a courthouse, City Hall, and a post office too,
and so it is said you can do anything here that you legally have to do.

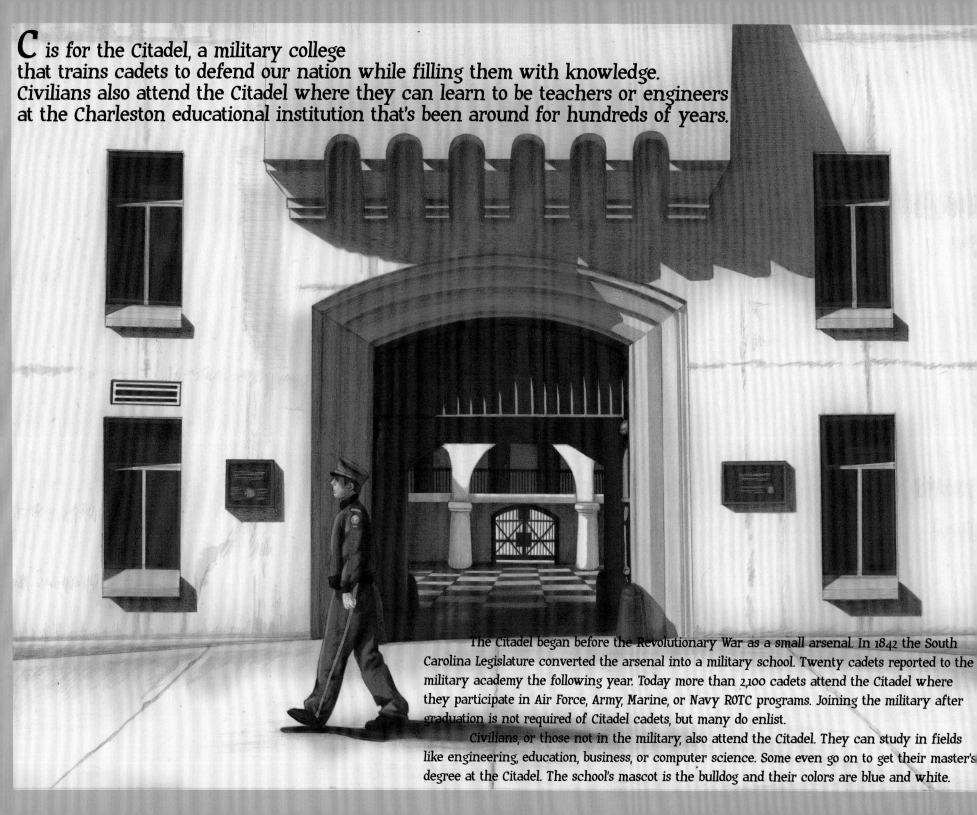

C is for the Citadel, a military college
that trains cadets to defend our nation while filling them with knowledge.
Civilians also attend the Citadel where they can learn to be teachers or engineers
at the Charleston educational institution that's been around for hundreds of years.

The Citadel began before the Revolutionary War as a small arsenal. In 1842 the South Carolina Legislature converted the arsenal into a military school. Twenty cadets reported to the military academy the following year. Today more than 2,100 cadets attend the Citadel where they participate in Air Force, Army, Marine, or Navy ROTC programs. Joining the military after graduation is not required of Citadel cadets, but many do enlist.

Civilians, or those not in the military, also attend the Citadel. They can study in fields like engineering, education, business, or computer science. Some even go on to get their master's degree at the Citadel. The school's mascot is the bulldog and their colors are blue and white.

D is for the dolphins, bottled-nosed and gray,
that live in Charleston Harbor where they jump, swim, and play.
Dolphins are very smart mammals, one of the smartest of all.
They use echolocation to find food, reading signals that bounce back
from their calls.

There are many fish and animals that depend on the waters of Charleston Harbor, but
perhaps none are as popular as the bottlenose dolphins. They are very intelligent creatures who
usually move in small groups called pods. They work together in these pods to hunt for the fish
they eat. The dolphins emit clicking noises and are able to detect the echoes from these clicks
that bounce off other fish in order to find them. Dolphins live all around the waters of Charleston.
Since they are mammals, not fish, and actually breathe air, they can be spotted from the beach or
in the harbor as they surface for more air.

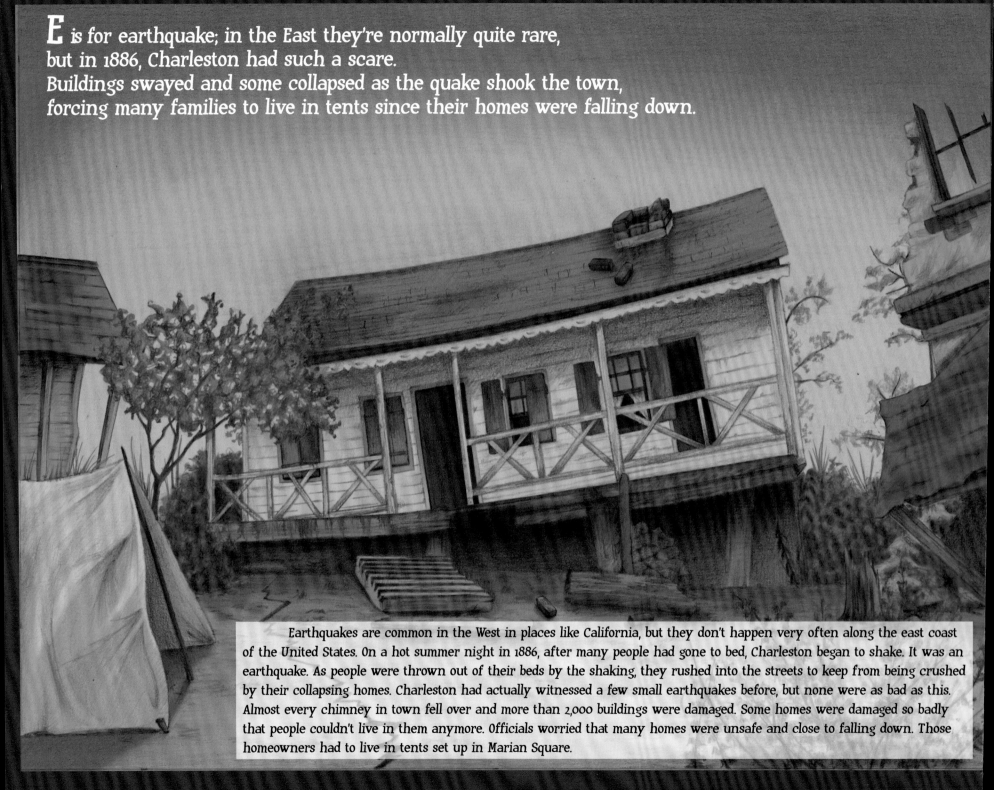

E is for earthquake; in the East they're normally quite rare,
but in 1886, Charleston had such a scare.
Buildings swayed and some collapsed as the quake shook the town,
forcing many families to live in tents since their homes were falling down.

Earthquakes are common in the West in places like California, but they don't happen very often along the east coast of the United States. On a hot summer night in 1886, after many people had gone to bed, Charleston began to shake. It was an earthquake. As people were thrown out of their beds by the shaking, they rushed into the streets to keep from being crushed by their collapsing homes. Charleston had actually witnessed a few small earthquakes before, but none were as bad as this. Almost every chimney in town fell over and more than 2,000 buildings were damaged. Some homes were damaged so badly that people couldn't live in them anymore. Officials worried that many homes were unsafe and close to falling down. Those homeowners had to live in tents set up in Marian Square.

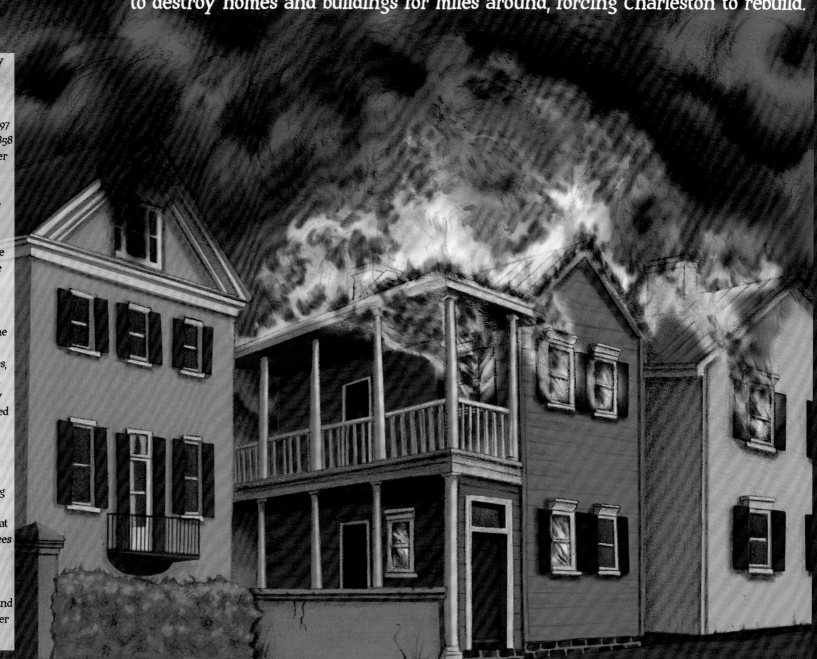

F is for the fire, burning hot and red.
With wooden homes so close together, the flames could quickly spread.
The town passed laws to keep them from starting, but fire kept coming still
to destroy homes and buildings for miles around, forcing Charleston to rebuild.

Throughout its early history, Charleston was very familiar with fire. No fewer than eight huge fires swept through the town between 1697 and 1876. Between 1825 and 1858 there were at least 204 smaller fires in Charleston. Many of those were caused by arson, meaning someone started the fires on purpose.

Many of the homes in Charleston during this time were made of wood and were built closely together. When a fire started, flames were able to quickly spread as wind blew glowing embers from one home to another. In an effort to combat the destructive fires, the town passed several laws. Some of these dealt with how a building could be constructed and what materials could be used for construction. Others outlawed certain activities within the city limits that involved fire, like soap-making or the use of fireworks. The city also issued new taxes that paid for fire protection services and equipment. Eventually, Charleston became better at preventing and fighting fire but not before many homes and businesses were destroyed over and over again.

The Gullah culture originated in West Africa. Africans were captured there and taken to American ports, usually in Charleston or Savannah, to be sold as slaves. These slaves could not always communicate with one another, and they certainly struggled to communicate with their English-speaking masters. In an effort to hold on to some of their African traditions and to communicate, the Gullah language and culture evolved among the slaves. They used the language to tell some of their African stories recast in American light and to sing some of their African songs.

Today, Gullah is still spoken by some people in coastal South Carolina and Georgia. The language has more English influences now than it did when the Africans first brought it to America, but it is still considered a separate language. Supreme Court Judge Clarence Thomas was raised as a Gullah speaker and many other native speakers have found success as well.

G is for Gullah, an old Lowcountry way
for slaves to keep African traditions as they worked and toiled each day.
Gullah is a culture and a language still spoken by some
who are reminded of their African roots and where they came from.

His for the most powerful storm, called a hurricane.
It's fed by the ocean's warm waters and produces high wind and rain.
Hugo was among the worst Charleston has seen, that was in 1989.
The city was destroyed and left with a mess of tree limbs and power lines.

All Atlantic Ocean hurricanes start as a tropical wave moving off the coast of Africa during the warmer months. As the tropical wave feeds off the warm waters of the ocean, it strengthens. If conditions are just right and the water temperature is warm enough, the storm can gain tremendous wind and rain potential.

A hurricane is rated on how fast its winds are moving. A category one hurricane has winds that are as fast as seventy-four miles per hour. The strongest hurricanes are rated as a category five and can have winds as fast as 155 miles per hour.

Charleston has witnessed many hurricanes over its history, but Hurricane Hugo which began making landfall on September 21, 1989, was the worst. A wall of water as high as seventeen feet washed over Fort Sumter. Nearly all the homes on Folly Beach were destroyed, and everywhere you looked, trees had fallen over and power lines lay tangled in the streets. The people of Charleston worked hard to rebuild the town and recover from the devastating storm.

I is for the islands within the Atlantic's reach,
where people have their homes or come to enjoy the beach.
Charleston's islands like James and Palm are surrounded on each side
by water that goes in and out according to the tide.

The Charleston area is home to several small barrier islands that are popular places to live or enjoy the beach. Sullivan's Island, Isle of Palm, James Island, Johns Island, Folly Beach, Kiawah Island, and Seabrook Island are just some of the islands in the Charleston area. They probably formed about 18,000 years ago as glaciers from an ice age melted and flooded areas behind beach ridges. Sediment deposited by the ocean and rivers carrying material from the mainland also helped construct them.

A barrier island's main function is to protect the mainland from powerful waves and winds caused by hurricanes and other strong storms. It also provides a habitat for the many animals and insects that live around the island. Many of these animals would not survive without the tides that rise and fall from the gravitational pull of the sun and moon.

Wadmalaw Island

Edisto Island

Seabroo Islan

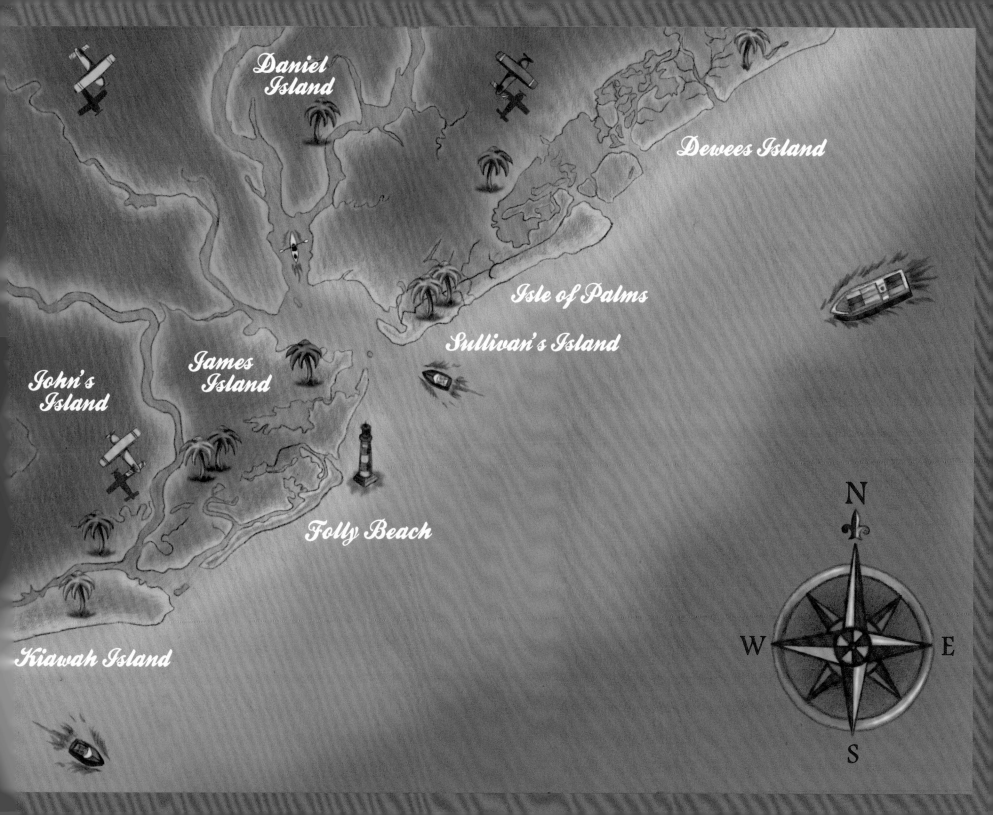

J is for jazz, the music from which would grow
the dance called the Charleston that the world would come to know.
The dance craze was started by Charleston's Jenkins Orphanage Band,
then adopted by the flappers who spread it across the land.

In the 1920s the Jazz Age arrived in Charleston. The music quickly grew popular around the city. The Rev. Daniel Jenkins operated an orphanage and wanted to take advantage of this trend. He had children from his orphanage stand on street corners and perform jazz in hopes that people passing by would donate coins. The Jenkins Orphanage Band wowed the people of Charleston, especially with the new and unique dance they created.

The flappers of the 1920s soon adopted the dance as their own. Flapper was a word used for some women who felt they should have more social equality with men and should be able to do more of things that they wanted. Back then it might not have been acceptable for a single woman to go out and dance to jazz music, and the flappers wanted to change that.

K is for the Kiawah Indians who lived here long before.

They grew crops and gathered shellfish along the marshy shore.

The Kiawah were of the Cusabo Indians along with ten other tribes or bands

who had lived for more than 4,000 years around the Lowcountry lands.

The Kiawah Indians were the first people to live in the Charleston area. They settled here as far back as 4,000 years ago. The Kiawah Indians, along with ten other tribes, made up the Cusabo Indians. The Cusabo ranged from the Savannah River to Charleston along the coast of the Atlantic Ocean. The Kiawah tribe lived on the land that is now Charleston. After the English colonists arrived, the Kiawah Tribe stopped most of their activities around the peninsula and Ashley River and spent much of their time on what is now Kiawah Island.

The Kiawah's favorite meal might have been oysters. The Indians walked through the marsh and gathered oysters wherever they could find them. Usually, they would eat the oysters as soon as they found them and then throw their shells on the ground. Throwing oyster shells on the ground for thousands of years made some big piles. These piles of shells are called middens, and such a midden at the tip of the Charleston Peninsula was one of the first things the English Colonists noticed when they sailed into the harbor. They named the area Oyster Point. Some oyster middens made by the Kiawah Indians can still be seen today.

L is for the landing where the English colonists first arrived in April of 1670 to make a colony they hoped would thrive. They named their settlement Charles Town in honor of the reigning king. New opportunity and a chance to be rich is what they hoped their colony would bring.

In April of 1670, a ship named the Carolina sailed into Charleston Harbor. Two other ships began the journey from England about seven months earlier along with the Carolina, but they were lost at sea. As the Carolina first entered the harbor, they saw Oyster Point. They continued sailing up the river they would later call Ashley. Eventually, the captain found a high patch of land on the western bank of the river and the colonists went ashore there.

They named that piece of land Albemarle Point which would later become Charles Towne Landing. They named their settlement Charles Towne in honor of King Charles II of England. He had granted the land to the colonists and eight lord proprietors who had invested in the colony hoping it would bring them vast wealth.

The Medical University of South Carolina started out in Charleston in 1824 as a small school for doctors. It is now the sixth oldest medical school in the country. When the school first started, it was very basic and offered doctors a general training in medicine. Now students can learn to be a pharmacist, a nurse, or a dentist. At one time only two students attended, but now more than 2,500 future health care providers are enrolled.

The MUSC Children's Hospital was built in 1987. This building serves everything from premature babies to teenagers. It is the only place in the region that can serve the most premature babies. It is known as one of the top pediatric hospitals in the whole country. The rest of MUSC's campus is spread across seventy-six acres and about ninety buildings.

M is for the Medical University of South Carolina, in short MUSC, where doctors and nurses come to learn how to help people like you and me. Here you can learn about the human body and all of its many ills. You can even learn to be a pharmacist, counting out your pills.

N is for the Northern forces who held Fort Sumter in their hands
when the first Confederate shot rang out and the Civil War began.
Confederate forces took the island fort, but the Union would soon take the town.
They launched mortar and rockets at the Southern troops who were determined to hold their ground.

By early April 1861, the stage for the Civil War was set. South Carolina had seceded from the Union, but Fort Sumter, sitting on an island in the middle of Charleston Harbor, was occupied by Major Robert Anderson and his Union troops. The Confederate forces in Charleston demanded that Major Anderson surrender. He refused, so in the early morning on April 12, 1861, Southern troops opened fire on Fort Sumter. The Civil War had begun. They continued firing upon the fort. Finally, nearly a day and a half later, Major Anderson was forced to surrender the Fort.

The tables were soon turned though as Northern forces took the city of Charleston. The stubborn Confederates refused to give up Fort Sumter and the island it sat on. For twenty-seven months, the Northern Forces fired rockets and missiles at the fort on a daily basis. The Confederates held their ground although they eventually had to give up the fort. Nevertheless, their determination to withstand the Union bombardment gave Charleston natives hope during a difficult time.

O is for the American opera titled *Porgy and Bess*.
An old Charleston neighborhood is where this opera is set.
The opera is based on a novel about an African-American man
trying to live in segregated Charleston and get by the best he can.

In 1935, George Gershwin's opera *Porgy and Bess* was first performed. The opera was based on the novel <u>Porgy</u> written by DuBose Heyward. The opera was slow to catch on in America but became popular in the late 1970s and mid 1980s when the Metropolitan Opera began to perform its classic pieces like "Summertime."

The story of the opera and novel center around a disabled African-American man named Porgy living in Charleston in a neighborhood called Catfish Row. Porgy tries to rescue Bess from other people in the neighborhood who are not nice to her. Porgy's story is believed to be based on a real Charleston citizen of the 1920s named Samuel Smalls who struggled as a black man in segregated Charleston. The neighborhood of Catfish Row was based on Cabbage Row, which is a real neighborhood in Charleston.

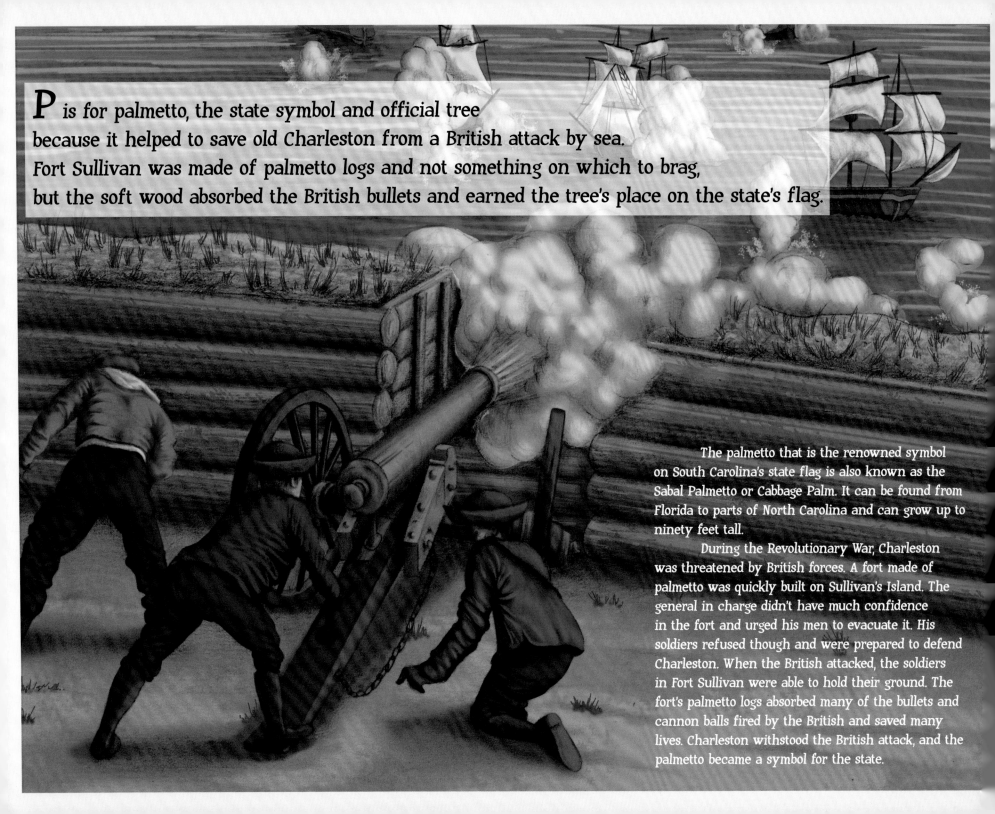

P is for palmetto, the state symbol and official tree
because it helped to save old Charleston from a British attack by sea.
Fort Sullivan was made of palmetto logs and not something on which to brag,
but the soft wood absorbed the British bullets and earned the tree's place on the state's flag.

The palmetto that is the renowned symbol on South Carolina's state flag is also known as the Sabal Palmetto or Cabbage Palm. It can be found from Florida to parts of North Carolina and can grow up to ninety feet tall.

During the Revolutionary War, Charleston was threatened by British forces. A fort made of palmetto was quickly built on Sullivan's Island. The general in charge didn't have much confidence in the fort and urged his men to evacuate it. His soldiers refused though and were prepared to defend Charleston. When the British attacked, the soldiers in Fort Sullivan were able to hold their ground. The fort's palmetto logs absorbed many of the bullets and cannon balls fired by the British and saved many lives. Charleston withstood the British attack, and the palmetto became a symbol for the state.

In May of 1718, Edward Thatch, better known as Blackbeard the Pirate, sailed his ship named *Queen Anne's Revenge* just outside Charleston Harbor. He and his crew of more than 300 men stopped every ship entering or leaving the port taking whatever goods they wanted. He also began kidnapping important Charleston dignitaries aboard the ships. In exchange for his prisoners' lives, Blackbeard demanded the governor of South Carolina give him a chest of medical supplies. After a couple of days of the blockade, the governor complied and sent out a small boat with the medicine. Clearly, some of Blackbeard's crew were ill. Normally, a pirate would have demanded gold or other riches. Some even think Blackbeard himself must have been sick to make such demands.

Q is for *Queen Anne's Revenge*, a powerful ship of war that belonged to Blackbeard the Pirate and his crew of 300 or more. They once took Charleston's harbor. They kidnapped and terrorized, but it wasn't gold they were after; they demanded medical supplies.

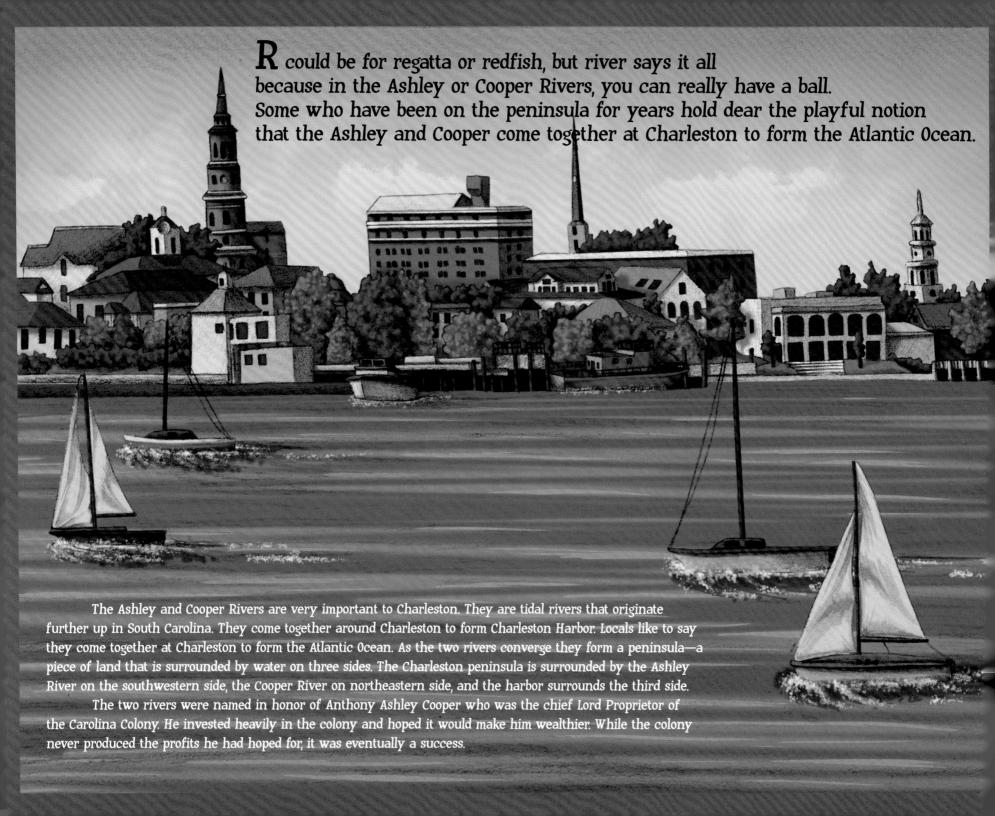

R could be for regatta or redfish, but river says it all
because in the Ashley or Cooper Rivers, you can really have a ball.
Some who have been on the peninsula for years hold dear the playful notion
that the Ashley and Cooper come together at Charleston to form the Atlantic Ocean.

The Ashley and Cooper Rivers are very important to Charleston. They are tidal rivers that originate
further up in South Carolina. They come together around Charleston to form Charleston Harbor. Locals like to say
they come together at Charleston to form the Atlantic Ocean. As the two rivers converge they form a peninsula—a
piece of land that is surrounded by water on three sides. The Charleston peninsula is surrounded by the Ashley
River on the southwestern side, the Cooper River on northeastern side, and the harbor surrounds the third side.
The two rivers were named in honor of Anthony Ashley Cooper who was the chief Lord Proprietor of
the Carolina Colony. He invested heavily in the colony and hoped it would make him wealthier. While the colony
never produced the profits he had hoped for, it was eventually a success.

S is for Spoleto, a festival of performing art
where many young and talented performers are able to get their start.
Based on an Italian tradition, it's one of the biggest events the town has.
Now this annual event features things like opera, theater, and jazz.

The Spoleto Festival, USA, first began in 1977. It is based on a similar festival held in Spoleto, Italy, called Festival dei Due Mondi, meaning the festival of two worlds. The festival brings an array of performing artists to Charleston every year over a two week period in May. These artists specialize in performing arts like opera, dance, theater, classical music, and jazz. One of the goals of the festival is to give new artists an opportunity to showcase their talents to other established performers and directors.

The loggerhead is the most common turtle found laying her eggs on Charleston area beaches. Between May and October these turtles crawl out of the Atlantic Ocean and onto the beach. Once there, they dig a hole in the sand and lay around 115 eggs. Then they bury their eggs in the sand and return to the ocean. About sixty days later, the baby turtles hatch from the eggs and emerge from the sand. They quickly scamper back to the ocean where they spend the rest of their lives. About twenty years later when the baby turtles are ready to lay their own eggs, they'll return to the same beach they were born on to build their own nests.

Unfortunately, many of the baby turtles do not survive to build their own nests. Some turtle nests are destroyed by raccoons, dogs running loose on the beach, or people. Lights from houses along the beach can confuse the baby turtles that are looking for the moon to guide them to the ocean. For the baby turtles that do make it to the ocean, there are many predators waiting for them there. Sea turtle watch groups work to find the nests along the beach and mark them so people can watch out for them.

T is for the turtles that dig their nests on summer nights
on Charleston's sandy beaches and fill them with spheres of white.
Mother turtle was born on this same beach, many years ago.
Her children will lay their own eggs here in twenty years or so.

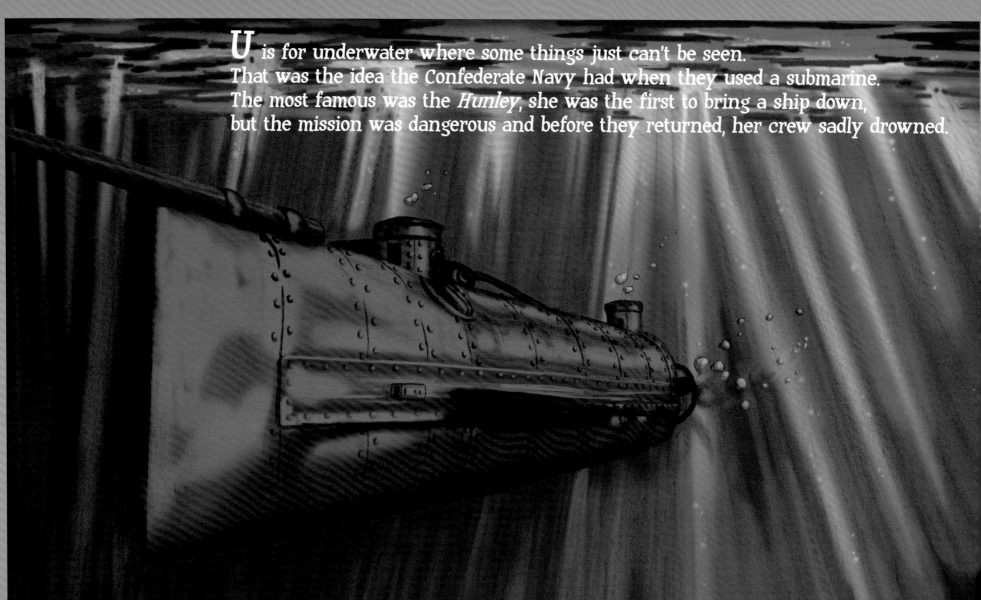

U is for underwater where some things just can't be seen.
That was the idea the Confederate Navy had when they used a submarine.
The most famous was the *Hunley*, she was the first to bring a ship down,
but the mission was dangerous and before they returned, her crew sadly drowned.

During the Civil War, a new idea was put into place—an underwater vessel or submarine used to attack other ships of war. The Confederate Navy hoped that a submarine could sneak underwater around Charleston Harbor and attack the Union ships in the area. The *David* was the first Confederate submarine to be used in combat. It didn't actually go underwater, but it did sit very low. It 1863, it attacked the *USS New Ironsides* in Charleston Harbor. Instead of a torpedo, it used an explosive charge stuck on the end of a long pole that it ran into the Union ship. *New Ironsides* didn't sink, but it was badly damaged.

The *CSS Hunley* was another Confederate submarine. Unlike The *David*, it was meant to go underwater but it was not submerged when it attacked the Union ship *Housatonic* in 1864. It also used an explosive charge on the end of a long pole. The *Hunley* rammed the *Housatonic*, then tried to retreat before the charge exploded. The *Housatonic* sank but the submarine was still too close when the charge went off and was damaged. The crew of the *Hunley* tried to get their vessel back to safety, but it sank and the crew drowned.

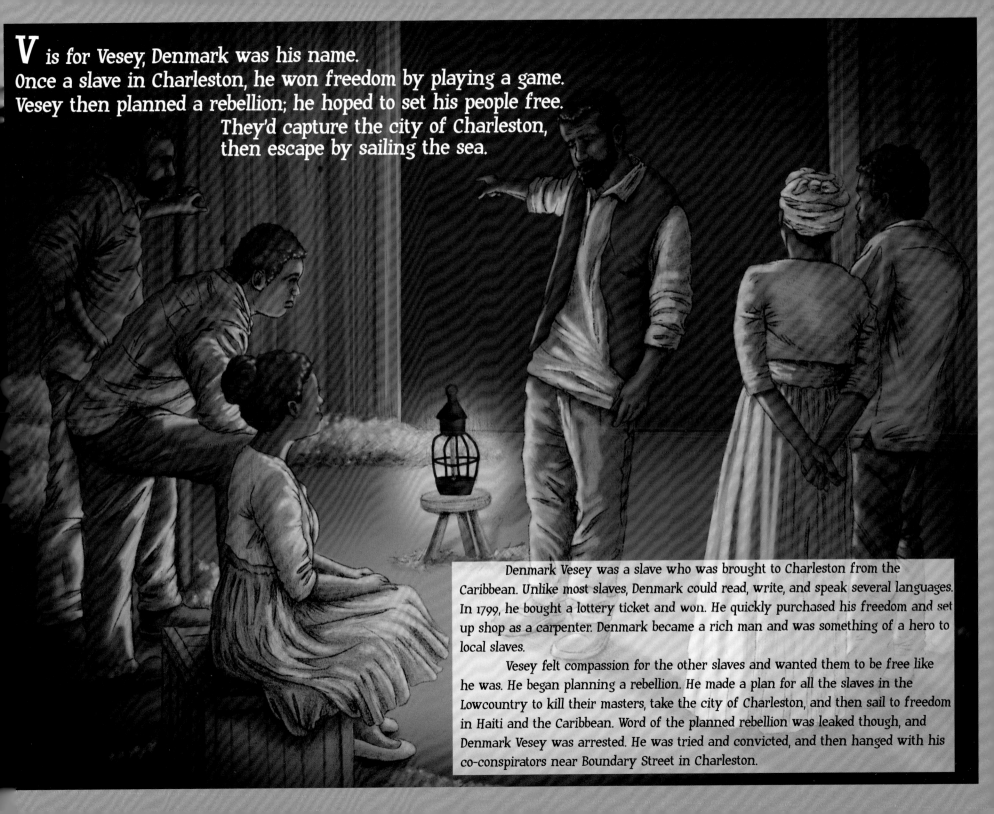

V is for Vesey, Denmark was his name.
Once a slave in Charleston, he won freedom by playing a game.
Vesey then planned a rebellion; he hoped to set his people free.
They'd capture the city of Charleston,
then escape by sailing the sea.

Denmark Vesey was a slave who was brought to Charleston from the Caribbean. Unlike most slaves, Denmark could read, write, and speak several languages. In 1799, he bought a lottery ticket and won. He quickly purchased his freedom and set up shop as a carpenter. Denmark became a rich man and was something of a hero to local slaves.

Vesey felt compassion for the other slaves and wanted them to be free like he was. He began planning a rebellion. He made a plan for all the slaves in the Lowcountry to kill their masters, take the city of Charleston, and then sail to freedom in Haiti and the Caribbean. Word of the planned rebellion was leaked though, and Denmark Vesey was arrested. He was tried and convicted, and then hanged with his co-conspirators near Boundary Street in Charleston.

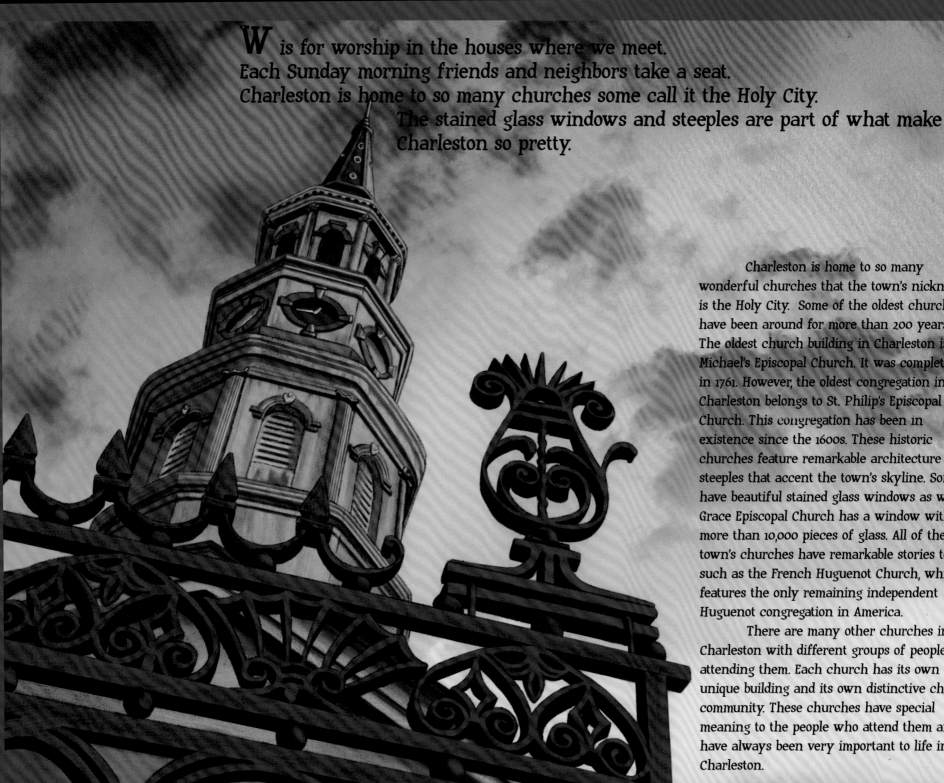

W is for worship in the houses where we meet.
Each Sunday morning friends and neighbors take a seat.
Charleston is home to so many churches some call it the Holy City.
The stained glass windows and steeples are part of what make
Charleston so pretty.

Charleston is home to so many wonderful churches that the town's nickname is the Holy City. Some of the oldest churches have been around for more than 200 years. The oldest church building in Charleston is St. Michael's Episcopal Church. It was completed in 1761. However, the oldest congregation in Charleston belongs to St. Philip's Episcopal Church. This congregation has been in existence since the 1600s. These historic churches feature remarkable architecture and steeples that accent the town's skyline. Some have beautiful stained glass windows as well. Grace Episcopal Church has a window with more than 10,000 pieces of glass. All of the town's churches have remarkable stories to tell such as the French Huguenot Church, which features the only remaining independent Huguenot congregation in America.

There are many other churches in Charleston with different groups of people attending them. Each church has its own unique building and its own distinctive church community. These churches have special meaning to the people who attend them and have always been very important to life in Charleston.

X comes from export, an activity at the port,
where ships go out and ships come in, carrying goods of every sort.
The port of Charleston is large and one of the busiest in the US.
It provides many local jobs and gives the economy zest.

The Port of Charleston is very important to the area. It is the second biggest source of revenue for the town behind tourism as it provides many jobs directly or indirectly. The port keeps area highways and rail lines very busy as well. Products that are produced in the United States are brought to Charleston by train or truck and then exported, or shipped out, to other ports all over the world. Products made in other places are imported, or shipped in, to Charleston, then carried by train or truck to other cities. Large container ships, capable of carrying thousands of tons of cargo enter the port every day of the year. Cruise ships also frequent the port. The Port of Charleston consistently ranks in the top ten for port activity in the United States.

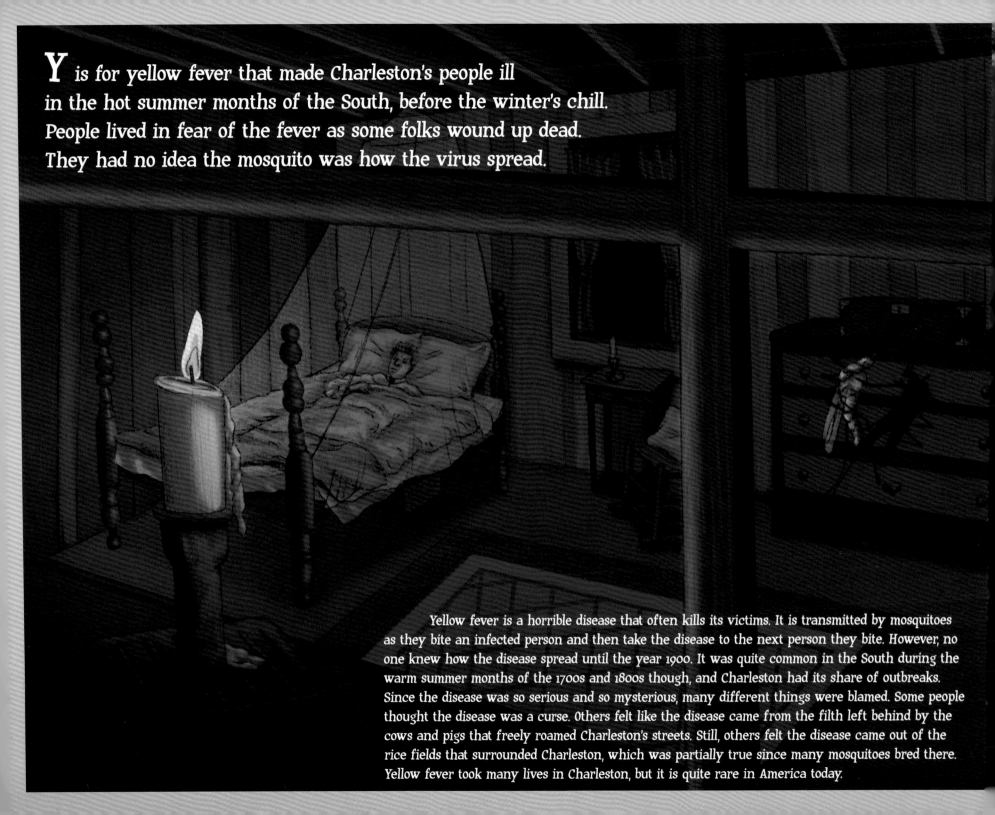

Y is for yellow fever that made Charleston's people ill
in the hot summer months of the South, before the winter's chill.
People lived in fear of the fever as some folks wound up dead.
They had no idea the mosquito was how the virus spread.

Yellow fever is a horrible disease that often kills its victims. It is transmitted by mosquitoes as they bite an infected person and then take the disease to the next person they bite. However, no one knew how the disease spread until the year 1900. It was quite common in the South during the warm summer months of the 1700s and 1800s though, and Charleston had its share of outbreaks. Since the disease was so serious and so mysterious, many different things were blamed. Some people thought the disease was a curse. Others felt like the disease came from the filth left behind by the cows and pigs that freely roamed Charleston's streets. Still, others felt the disease came out of the rice fields that surrounded Charleston, which was partially true since many mosquitoes bred there. Yellow fever took many lives in Charleston, but it is quite rare in America today.

Z is from azalea and Charleston A to Z.
Like these flowers full of color, Charleston is full of history.
These flowers are so beautiful and abundant during the spring,
as abundant as the pleasures Charleston is sure to bring.

The azalea is a flowering shrub that is native to the southeastern United States. They can grow over ten feet tall. Around Charleston, the plant is very popular in lawns and gardens. In the winter the azalea makes a nice green bush, but its real charm comes in the spring. Usually between February and April the plant blooms with hundreds of brightly colored flowers. The flowers last just a couple of weeks, but they are a sight to see as they flourish on Charleston's lawns.

Charleston and the Lowcountry is a wonderful place. Whether you live here or are just visiting, you can't help but to appreciate all the town has to offer. From its deep history to the rich activities it offers people today, Charleston truly is a remarkable place to visit and live.